Time-Tested Southern Appetizers Cookbook

Authentic and Super Tasty Southern Comfort Finger Food Recipes

The Southern Table

By

Rola Oliver

Copyright © 2023 by Rola Oliver

License Notice

I'm from the south and we don't like to sugarcoat things there. That's why I prefer to get straight to the point here, which is the copyright license in this book.

While it probably isn't the first time you stumble upon the legend, here it is again in case you've forgotten: Do not make any print or electronic reproductions, sell, re-publish, or distribute this book in parts or as a whole unless you have express written consent from me or my team.

Please help me protect my work so I can continue funding future projects by respecting the copyright, otherwise I'll have to spend more time in court than in my kitchen whipping up delicious new recipes!

Big hugs,

Rola O.

Table of Contents

Introduction 6

Gameday Recipes 8

   1. Sausage and Biscuit Roll Ups 9

   2. Beefy Tailgating Nachos 11

   3. Baked Footballin Onion Rings 13

   4. Hot Dog Nachos 15

   5. Maple Pecans 17

   6. Black Bean Guac 19

Snack Recipes 21

   7. Hush Puppies 22

   8. Mini Tomato Pies 24

   9. Butternut Squash Fries 26

   10. Louisiana Garlic Knots 28

   11. October Whoopie Pies 30

   12. Rosemary Meatballs 32

   13. Jalapeno Poppers 34

   14. Cheesy Corn Meal Balls 36

   15. Potato Pots 38

   16. Caliente Deviled Eggs 40

   17. Cracker Bruschetta 42

18. Kentucky Brown Bites 44

19. Marinated Shrimp and Pineapple 46

20. Wonton Crackers 48

21. Baked Shrimp Skewers 50

22. Mushroom Cups 52

23. Applesauce Doughnut Holes 54

24. Sweet Biscuits 56

25. Southern Fried Chicken Toast 58

26. Carolina Biscuits 60

27. Greek Spinach Bars 62

28. Southern Fried Mushrooms 64

29. Kielbasa Cups 66

30. Bacon Bits and Pimento Cheese Hors D'oeuvres 68

31. Pimento Deviled Eggs 70

Fritter Recipes 72

32. Fall Fritters 73

33. Corn Fritters 75

34. Cajun Fritters 77

35. Happy as Clams Fritters 79

36. Appalachian Trail Fritters 81

37. Florida Fritters 83

38. Gulf Coast Fritters 85

39. Autumns Apple Fritters 87

Dip Recipes 89

40. Herbed Blue Cheese Spread 90

41. Savory Onion Dip 92

42. South Florida Fish Dip 94

43. Big Bend Shrimp Dip 96

44. Baked Spinach Dip 98

45. Pimento Cheese Spread 100

46. Creamy Turnip Dip 102

47. Salsa Substitute 104

48. Cauliflower Hummus 106

49. Beer Dip 108

50. Lima Bean Guac 110

Author's Afterthoughts 112

Introduction

In addition to the traditional tailgate party, you could also consider hosting a Southern-themed dinner party for a more intimate gathering. Start off with a classic shrimp and grits appetizer, followed by a main course of crispy fried chicken or slow-cooked pulled pork. For sides, consider serving up some creamy mac and cheese, Southern-style collard greens, and buttery cornbread.

For dessert, why not try making a decadent chocolate pecan pie or a creamy banana pudding? And for drinks, you could offer up some classic Southern cocktails like a whiskey sour or a mint julep.

To really set the mood, consider decorating your dining room with some Southern-inspired décor, such as mason jar centerpieces and rustic wooden accents. And don't forget to play some classic Southern tunes to really get your guests in the mood!

Whether you're hosting a tailgate party or a dinner party, Southern cuisine is the perfect way to bring people together and celebrate good food, good drinks, and good company. So break out your apron, fire up the stove, and get ready to impress your guests with some delicious Southern dishes.

wwwwwwwwwwwwwwwwwwwwwww

Gameday Recipes

wwwwwwwwwwwwwwwwwwwwww

1. Sausage and Biscuit Roll Ups

Serve: 10

Ingredient List:

- 1 roll of frozen biscuits
- 10 sausage cocktail franks
- 1 tbsp. of cayenne pepper
- 1 tbsp. of butter, melted
- 1 package of cheddar cheese

wwwwwwwwwwwwwwwwwwwwww

How to Cook:

i. In a pot , melt butter and stir in the cayenne pepper, roll out the dough and flatten to approx. 1-2 inches thick, brush butter mixture onto dough, sprinkle cheese over the entire thing, cut into thin strips, and wrap around cocktail frank.

ii. Bake for a period of 10 minutes at a temperature of 400°F or until the dough is golden brown and the cheese has melted.

2. Beefy Tailgating Nachos

Serve: 1 9x9 tray

Ingredient List:

- 1 bag of fav low sodium tortilla chips or homemade tortilla chips
- 2-3 cups of worth shredded roast beef or London broil
- 1 cup of white cheddar cheese
- 1/3 cup of diced jalapenos
- 1 jar, drained, roasted red peppers
- 1-2 diced avocados
- 2 tsp. of celery salt

wwwwwwwwwwwwwwwwwwwwwww

How to Cook:

i. Preheat the oven to a temperature of 350°F and prepare a 9x9 baking dish.

ii. Layout chips in the bottom of the dish, and top with beef, cheese, peppers, avocados, and spices, bake for a period of 20-25 minutes or until cheese is melted.

iii. If brown bubbles on the cheese are desired, stick it under the broiler for a period of 2-3 minutes.

3. Baked Footballin Onion Rings

Serve: 24

Ingredient List:

- 1 onion cut into 24 rings
- All-purpose flour
- 1/2 tbsp. of chili powder
- 1/4 tsp. of jalapeno powder
- 1/3 tsp. of celery salt
- 1/3 tsp. of black pepper
- 1 tbsp. of plain breadcrumbs
- Olive oil spray

wwwwwwwwwwwwwwwwwwwwwww

How to Cook:

i. Preheat the oven to a temperature of 350°F, and prepare a baking tray.

ii. In a bowl mix together ingredients 2-6, dip the onions in them ensuring an even light coating and layout on the tray, mist with spray, and bake for a period of 25-30 minutes.

4. Hot Dog Nachos

Serve: a 9x9 dish

Ingredient List:

- 1 package of hot dogs, sliced into pieces
- 1 package of tater tots or hash browns
- Wonton crackers (see recipe in Snacks)
- 1 package of shredded cheddar cheese
- 1/2 tsp. of chili powder
- 1/2 tsp. of celery salt
- 1 can of diced tomatoes and green chilies, drained
- 1/3 cup of chopped jalapeno or 1/2 tsp. jalapeno powder
- 1/3 cup of chopped black olives

wwwwwwwwwwwwwwwwwwwwwww

How to Cook:

i. Preheat the oven to a temperature of 350°F and prepare a 9x9 dish

ii. Place wonton crackers in the bottom of a 9x9 dish, and top with hot dog slices, tater tots or hash browns, cheese, spices, tomatoes & chilies, jalapenos, and olives.

iii. Bake for a period of 30 minutes or until the cheese has melted.

5. Maple Pecans

Serve: 2 cups

Ingredient List:

- 2 cups of shelled pecans
- 2 cups of maple syrup
- 1/4 tsp. of salt
- 1 tsp. of chili pepper
- 1/2 tbsp. of butter

wwwwwwwwwwwwwwwwwwwwwwww

How to Cook:

i. Over medium heat mix syrup, salt, and chili pepper, into melted butter, pour in nuts and stir making sure all are coated.

ii. Spoon out, letting excess syrup run off, lay on the tray and chill for a period of 1 hr.

6. Black Bean Guac

Serve: 2-3 cups

Ingredient List:

- 1 can of black beans washed and drained
- 1 diced bell pepper
- 1 can of whole kernel corn washed and drained
- 2 diced avocados
- 1/2 diced sweet onion
- 1/2 tbsp. of garlic salt
- 1 cup of cheddar cheese
- Scallions or parsley (optional)

wwwwwwwwwwwwwwwwwwwwwww

How to Cook:

i. Mix everything together in a bowl and either chill in an airtight container or warm in the oven and melt the cheese

Snack Recipes

wwwwwwwwwwwwwwwwwwwwww

7. Hush Puppies

Serve: 12

Ingredient List:

- 3 eggs
- 1 1/4 cups of buttermilk
- 1/3 cup of vegetable oil
- 1 1/4 cups of all-purpose flour AND cornmeal
- 2 tsp. of sugar
- 1/2 tsp. of baking powder
- 1 tbsp. of minced onion
- 1 tsp. of minced thyme
- oil for frying

wwwwwwwwwwwwwwwwwwwwwww

How to Cook:

i. In one bowl mix together eggs, buttermilk, and oil; in another bowl mix together, flour, cornmeal, sugar, baking powder, onion, and thyme.

ii. Fold the wet ingredients into the dry ingredients and mix together well. Take a tbsp. worth of dough, roll it into a ball and flatten it into a plump disc then fry until golden brown.

iii. For Southwestern or Tex Mex flare add 1/3 tbsp. chili or cayenne pepper, corn, and/or diced jalapeno or chipotle peppers

8. Mini Tomato Pies

Serve: 10-12

Ingredient List:

- 1 roll of frozen croissant dough
- 1/2 tbsp. of butter, melted
- 1 tbsp. of brown sugar
- 2/3 tbsp. of olive oil
- 1 can of diced onion and garlic tomatoes
- 1 cup of crumbled feta cheese
- 1 tbsp. of EACH: diced basil AND thyme
- 1/3 tsp. of orange peel

wwwwwwwwwwwwwwwwwwwwww

How to Cook:

i. Roll out and flatten the dough, take just enough dough to cover the bottom and sides of muffin molds: melt butter adding brown sugar and olive oil then brush onto muffin bottoms, saving any remaining liquid for later use: bake at a temperature of 400°F for a period of 6-8 minutes or until set.

ii. In a large bowl mix remaining ingredients, and any remaining butter mix, together and spoon into muffin molds, bake at a temperature of 350°F for another period of 6-10 minutes

9. Butternut Squash Fries

Serve: 20-24

Ingredient List:

- 2-4 cups of butternut squash cut into French fry shape
- 1/3 tsp. of black pepper
- 1/2 tsp. of smoked paprika
- 1/6 tsp. of sea salt
- Olive oil spray

wwwwwwwwwwwwwwwwwwwwwwww

How to Cook:

i. Preheat the oven to a temperature of 425°F and prepare the baking tray.

ii. In a bowl mix together seasonings and toss fries in it ensuring a good even coating; layout on the tray, mist with spray, and bake for a period of 30 minutes.

10. Louisiana Garlic Knots

Serve: 20

Ingredient List:

- 1 roll of frozen pizza dough
- 1/2 cup of shredded provolone
- 1/3 cup of shredded mozzarella
- 1/4 tsp. of onion powder
- 1/2 cup of diced mushroom
- 1/2 cup of diced tomatoes and green chilies, drained of as much juice as possible
- 1 tbsp. of melted butter
- 1 tsp. of garlic powder and parsley

wwwwwwwwwwwwwwwwwwwwwww

How to Cook:

i. Preheat the oven to a temperature of 425°F and prepare muffin molds.

ii. Mix the dough as directed, taking 1 tbsp. a sized piece spread into the bottom of a muffin mold and up the sides.

iii. In another bowl mix together cheeses, onion powder, mushrooms, tomatoes and chilies, spoon 1/2 spoon of it into the dough and cover with that on the sides of molds.

iv. Bake for a period of 8-12 minutes; meanwhile, put butter and garlic/parsley powder into a microwave-safe dish and melt then pour over knots.

11. October Whoopie Pies

Serve: 12-15

pg. 30

Ingredient List:

- 1 cup of brown sugar
- 1 cup of pumpkin puree
- 2/3 cup of veg. oil
- 2 egg yolks
- 2 1/2 cups of all-purpose flour
- 1/2 tsp. of EACH: salt, vanilla extract, baking soda
- 1/4 tsp. of baking powder
- 2/3 tbsp. of EACH: cinnamon and ginger
- 1/2 tbsp. of cloves
- 1 egg white
- 1 tbsp. of milk
- 1/2 cup of shortening
- 1 1/3 cups of confectioners' sugar

wwwwwwwwwwwwwwwwwwwwwww

How to Cook:

i. Combine brown sugar, pumpkin, oil, yolks, flour, salt, vanilla, baking powder & soda, cinnamon, ginger, and cloves.

ii. Form into balls approx. the size of a tsp. and bake for a period of 9-13 minutes at a temperature of 350°F.

For the cream: beat egg, milk, shortening, and sugar

12. Rosemary Meatballs

Serve: 30

Ingredient List:

- 1 diced shallot
- 4 finely diced sprigs of rosemary, approx. 1-1 1/2 tbsp.
- 2 eggs
- 1/3 cup of breadcrumbs or panko
- 2 tbsp. of ricotta cheese
- 1/3 cup of beef bullion
- 1/2 pound of ground beef
- 2 cups of fav bbq sauce
- 1/2 tsp. of sriracha sauce

wwwwwwwwwwwwwwwwwwwwwww

How to Cook:

i. Preheat the oven to a temperature of 400°F and prepare the baking tray.

ii. Mix all ingredients together except bbq and sriracha sauce, form into balls and lay out on a tray, and bake for a period of 45-55 minutes.

iii. In a Dutch oven over low heat put baked meatballs into warm bbq & sriracha sauce and let simmer.

13. Jalapeno Poppers

Serve: 10

Ingredient List:

- 5 jalapenos, halved and cleaned
- 1 block of cream cheese
- 1 tsp. of diced parsley
- 1/4 cup of diced chicken
- Breadcrumbs
- Parmesan cheese
- 5 slices of Prosciutto

wwwwwwwwwwwwwwwwwwwwwww

How to Cook:

i. Soak toothpicks before sticking them in the oven, preheat the oven to a temperature of 400 °Fand prepare the baking tray.

ii. In a small bowl mix together cream cheese, parsley, and chicken; cut cleaned jalapenos in half and fill with cream cheese mixture.

iii. Top with breadcrumbs and cheese then wrap in prosciutto and pin with a wet toothpick and bake for a period of 30 minutes.

14. Cheesy Corn Meal Balls

Serve: 10

Ingredient List:

- 1 cup of cornmeal
- 1 tbsp. of Italian breadcrumbs
- 1 egg white
- 1/4 cup of milk
- 1 tbsp. of Parmesan cheese

wwwwwwwwwwwwwwwwwwwwwwww

How to Cook:

i. Preheat the oven to a temperature of 350°F and prepare the baking tray.

ii. Mix the ingredients together, form them into balls, and bake for a period of 20-25 minutes.

15. Potato Pots

Serve: 10

Ingredient List:

- 10 small potatoes
- Olive oil spray
- 3 oz. of cream cheese
- 1 tbsp. of sour cream
- 3/4 tsp. of Italian seasoning
- 1 1/2 cups of whole-kernel corn
- 1/4 cup of crumbled feta cheese

wwwwwwwwwwwwwwwwwwwwwww

How to Cook:

i. Preheat the oven to a temperature of 350°F and prepare a baking tray.

ii. Layout cleaned potatoes on a tray, spray with oil and bake at 400° for a period of 30-35 minutes: let potatoes cool for a period of 15-20 minutes before handling.

iii. Turn the oven temp up to 425°F, cut the potatoes in half, scoop out the potatoes, mist the insides with spray, and cook for a period of 6-8 minutes.

iv. Place potato pulp in a large bowl along with all other ingredients. Mix well and spoon into potato shells.

16. Caliente Deviled Eggs

Serve: 20

Ingredient List:

- 10 hard-boiled eggs
- Spicy mustard
- 10 jalapenos
- 1/3 tbsp. of smoked paprika
- 4-5 diced scallions

wwwwwwwwwwwwwwwwwwwwwwww

How to Cook:

i. Peel and cut eggs in half, lay face-up on a tray, and put yolks in a large mixing bowl along with mustard, jalapeno, and smoked paprika.

ii. Mash yolks and incorporate into a mix and spoon into eggs, top with scallion pieces, and chill for at least a period of 30-40 minutes.

17. Cracker Bruschetta

Serve: 20

Ingredient List:

- 20-round butter crackers
- 8 sliced cherry tomatoes
- Diced bruschetta
- 20 2x2 slices of mozzarella
- 2/3 cup of olive oil
- 1/4 cup of red wine vinegar
- 1 tbsp. of diced rosemary

wwwwwwwwwwwwwwwwwwwwwww

How to Cook:

i. Mix olive oil, red wine vinegar, and rosemary together and let it sit in the refrigerator for a period of one hour.

ii. Layout the crackers on a tray, and top each with one slice of cheese, one slice of tomato, and bruschetta.

iii. Drizzle each one with rosemary vinaigrette.

18. Kentucky Brown Bites

Serve: 24

Ingredient List:

- 1 package of puff pastry cups
- 1 package of bruschetta, diced
- 1 package of deli turkey, diced
- 1/2 cup of milk
- 1/2 tbsp. of butter
- 3/4 cup of flour
- 1/4 tsp. of black pepper
- 1/2 tbsp. of diced basil
- 1/2 tbsp. of diced parsley
- 3 oz. provolone cheese
- 3 oz. of white cheddar cheese
- 24 pieces of parsley, diced scallions diced peppers, or diced mushrooms

wwwwwwwwwwwwwwwwwwwwww

How to Cook:

i. Preheat the oven to a temperature of 350°F and prepare mini muffin molds.

ii. Place pastry cups in the mold: in a Dutch oven over high heat melt butter into milk, slowly stir in flour, and add spices, seasonings, diced turkey, diced bruschetta, and cheese. Stir until well blended and smooth, and turn the heat to low (this will keep the cheese from congealing)

iii. Add 1/2 spoonful of the cheese sauce into cups, and bake for a period of 25-30 minutes.

19. Marinated Shrimp and Pineapple

Serve: 5

Ingredient List:

- 20 shrimp: cleaned, shelled, deveined, and detailed
- 20 pieces of chopped pineapple, cut into 3x3 squares
- 2 diced onions
- 1 diced red bell pepper
- 1 tbsp. of low-sodium soy sauce
- 1 cup of pineapple juice
- 1/2 tbsp. of brown sugar
- 1/2 tbsp. of honey
- 5 wet skewers

wwwwwwwwwwwwwwwwwwwwww

How to Cook:

i. Soak skewers for thirty minutes before sticking them in the grill.

ii. In a plastic bag place all ingredients and marinate for a period of 25-20 minutes.

iii. Remove and stick on skewers, and grill for a period of 5-8 minutes on each side or until shrimp is no longer pink.

iv. Don't worry, or consider them burned, if they get grill marks.

20. Wonton Crackers

Serve: 20

Ingredient List:

- 20 wonton wrappers
- 1/3 tbsp. of sea salt
- 1 tsp. of orange peel
- oil for frying

wwwwwwwwwwwwwwwwwwwwwwww

How to Cook:

i. Fold the wanton in a triangle shape, fry till golden brown (approx. for a period of 20 seconds on each side), remove, and layout separately, letting cool on a baking tray.

ii. In a small bowl mix together salt and orange peel then sprinkle over wontons

iii. To bake layout wontons on a parchment lined tray, spray or drizzle with oil, and bake for a period of 25-30 minutes at a temperature of 350°F.

21. Baked Shrimp Skewers

Serve: 6

Ingredient List:

- 24 shrimp, clean, deveined, and detailed
- 1 cup of flour
- 1/3 cup of plain breadcrumbs
- 1/4 tsp. of smoked paprika
- Wet bamboo skewers
- Olive oil spray

wwwwwwwwwwwwwwwwwwwwwwww

How to Cook:

i. Soak skewers for thirty minutes, preheat the oven to a temperature of 350°F, and prepare a baking tray.

ii. In a bowl mix together flour, breadcrumbs, and spice; roll shrimp in mix coating evenly but lightly; put 4 on each skewer and mist with spray, and bake for a period of 15-20 minutes.

22. Mushroom Cups

Serve: 24

Ingredient List:

- 1 package of mini puff pastry cups
- 4 oz. of cream cheese
- 1/2 cup of diced mushroom pieces
- 1/2 diced bell peppers or jalapenos
- 2 oz. of Parmesan cheese
- 1 tbsp. of finely diced EACH: parsley, oregano, mint and thyme

wwwwwwwwwwwwwwwwwwwwwwww

How to Cook:

i. Preheat the oven to a temperature of 350°F and prepare mini muffin molds.

ii. Place cups in molds, in a bowl mix together the remaining ingredients, spoon into each cup filling approx. 2/3 and bake for a period of 20-30 minutes.

23. Applesauce Doughnut Holes

Serve: 12

Ingredient List:

- oil for frying
- 1 cup self-rising flour
- 1/4 tsp. of apple pie seasoning
- 1/6 tsp. of nutmeg
- 1/6 tsp. of cloves
- 1 tbsp. of brown sugar
- 1 tbsp. of white sugar
- 2 egg whites
- 1/3 cup of milk
- 2/3 cup of applesauce
- 1 tsp. of vanilla extract or 2 vanilla beans

wwwwwwwwwwwwwwwwwwwwwww

How to Cook:

i. Mix ingredients 2-6 together, fold in applesauce and vanilla, and drop by rounded tsp. into the hot oil.

ii. Fry for a period of 2-4 minutes or until golden brown.

24. Sweet Biscuits

Serve: 20

Ingredient List:

- 2 cups of worth of cooked sweet potato pulp or mash
- 3/4 cup of buttermilk
- 1/2 tsp. of vanilla extract
- 1-2 tbsp. of butter
- 1/2 tbsp. of brown sugar
- 2-3 cups of self-rising flour

wwwwwwwwwwwwwwwwwwwwwww

How to Cook:

i. With flour, start with 2 cups and slowly work your way up to 3 (1 tbsp. at a time) if needed

ii. Put all the ingredients into a bowl and mix well, dump onto a floured surface, and knead for a period of 45 seconds then roll it into a log.

iii. Wrap in clear wrap or parchment paper and chill for a period of 10 minutes, remove and cut into rounds; layout on the baking tray and cook at a temperature of 400°F for a period of 15-20 minutes (time will also depend on thickness so check every few minutes until the exact time is known)

25. Southern Fried Chicken Toast

Serve: 12

Ingredient List:

- 1 boneless, skinless, chicken breasts or thighs, diced or shredded and cooked
- 1/3 cup of diced tomatoes with green chilies, drained
- 1/2 tbsp. of brown sugar
- 1/3 tsp. of celery salt
- 1/3 cup of provolone or mozzarella cheese
- 1 tbsp. of melted butter
- 1/2 tbsp. of oil for cooking
- 3 pieces of white bread cut into 12 squares or triangles

wwwwwwwwwwwwwwwwwwwwwww

How to Cook:

i. Place the first four ingredients into a bowl and mix; melt butter and pour 1/2 tbsp. into the mix.

ii. Pour the remaining butter into the skillet along with 1/2 tbsp. of oil and let it heat up.

iii. Working in batches of 3 or 4 spoon chicken mix onto bread and place into skillet, top with cheese, and let cook 5-6 minutes

26. Carolina Biscuits

Serve: 20

Ingredient List:

- 20 sweet potato biscuits
- 1 package of coleslaw or broccoli slaw
- 3 cups worth of pulled pork meat
- Fav bbq sauce

wwwwwwwwwwwwwwwwwwwwwww

How to Cook:

i. On a tray layout biscuit, top with 1/2 tbsp. of coleslaw or broccoli slaw, place approx. 1 tbsp. worth of pulled pork on top of slaw and covered with 1- 2 tsp. of sauce.

ii. If desired warm in the oven at a temperature of 200°F.

27. Greek Spinach Bars

Serve: an 11x9 dish of approx. 15-18 bars

Ingredient List:

- 2 tbsp. of olive oil
- 1 diced shallot
- 4-5 scallions, diced
- 1 tbsp. of minced garlic
- 4 cups of chopped spinach
- 1/2 tbsp. of EACH: thyme and oregano
- 4 eggs
- 1 cup of EACH: feta cheese, ricotta cheese, and mozzarella
- 1 package of phyllo dough
- Olive oil for brushing

wwwwwwwwwwwwwwwwwwwwwwww

How to Cook:

i. Preheat the oven to a temperature of 400°F and prepare an 11x9 dish.

ii. Sauté shallot, scallions, and garlic; add spinach and stir for 3 minutes or until it begins to wilt, remove from heat and let cool down. In another bowl mix together eggs, spices, cheeses and gradually stir the spinach mix into it. Lay strips of dough in the dish and brush with oil, repeat 3 times, pour spinach mix into the dish over the dough evenly and cover with remaining dough also brushing with oil.

iii. Bake for a period of 25-28 minutes.

28. Southern Fried Mushrooms

Serve: 12

Ingredient List:

- 12 mushrooms, cleaned and dried
- oil for frying
- 1/3 cup of red cooking wine
- 3 tsp. of water
- 1 cup of all-purpose flour
- 1/4 tbsp. of minced garlic
- 1 dash of onion powder
- Mozzarella cheese
- 1 tbsp. of Italian breadcrumbs

wwwwwwwwwwwwwwwwwwwwwww

How to Cook:

i. Mix together wine, water, garlic, and onion powder in a plastic bag and marinate the mushrooms for a period of 30 minutes.

ii. Mix together flour, cheese shreds, and breadcrumbs, dip the mushrooms in the mix, coating well and evenly then dip into hot oil and fry for a period of 4-6 minutes.

29. Kielbasa Cups

Serve: 24

Ingredient List:

- 1 recipe of pimento spread (see Dip-Spread section for recipe)
- 24 phyllo mini cups
- 2 packs of kielbasa sausage, diced

wwwwwwwwwwwwwwwwwwwwwwwww

How to Cook:

i. Preheat the oven to a temperature of 425°F and prepare mini muffin molds.

ii. Place cups into molds, place a few pieces of kielbasa, and cover with pimento spread.

iii. Bake for a period of 12-15 minutes.

30. Bacon Bits and Pimento Cheese Hors D'oeuvres

Serve: 14-18

Ingredient List:

- 1 recipe of pimento cheese spread
- 4-5 pieces of bacon finely diced
- 2 cups of breadcrumbs

wwwwwwwwwwwwwwwwwwwwwwww

How to Cook:

i. Preheat the oven to a temperature of 350°F and prepare a baking tray

ii. In a large bowl mix bacon bits into pimento cheese spread, and roll a tbsp. worth of dough into a ball and roll in breadcrumbs.

iii. Layout them on a tray and bake for a period of 12-15 minutes or until the bacon is done.

31. Pimento Deviled Eggs

Serve: 20

Ingredient List:

- 20 hard boiled eggs, halved and emptied
- 1 recipe of pimento spread
- 1/2 cup of bacon bits (optional)
- Diced scallions, chives, or parsley for garnish (optional)

wwwwwwwwwwwwwwwwwwwwwww

How to Cook:

i. Spoon pimento mix into egg half as you would with normal deviled eggs, cover, and refrigerate at least a period of 40 minutes before serving

Fritter Recipes

32. Fall Fritters

These simple treats go great with coffee!

Serve: 12

Ingredient List:

- 1 cup of all-purpose flour
- 1/2 tsp. of baking powder
- 1 egg
- 1 cup of pumpkin puree
- 1/4 tsp. of cinnamon
- 1/4 tsp. of cloves

wwwwwwwwwwwwwwwwwwwwwwww

How to Cook:

i. In a bowl mix together flour, baking powder, eggs, pumpkin, cinnamon, and cloves; take 1/2 tbsp. worth of dough, form it into a ball, and fry until golden brown for a period of 1-3 minutes.

33. Corn Fritters

Lots of room for personal touches here!

Serve: 12

Ingredient List:

- 1 cup of all-purpose flour
- 2/3 tsp. of baking powder
- 1/2 tsp. of sugar
- 1 egg
- 1/3 + 1 tbsp. of milk
- 2/3 tbsp. of butter, melted
- 1/2 12 ounces. can of whole-kernel corn
- oil for frying

wwwwwwwwwwwwwwwwwwwwwww

How to Cook:

i. In a bowl mix together flour and baking powder; in another bowl, mix together sugar, egg, milk, and butter.

ii. Fold the dry ingredients into the wet and stir, add corn and mix thoroughly, take 1/2 tbsp. of dough, form it into a ball, and fry for a period of 1-3 minutes on each side or until golden brown.

iii. Remember not to make individual fritters too big or they will not cook through

34. Cajun Fritters

Serve: 12

Ingredient List:

- 1 cup of all-purpose flour
- 2/3 tsp. of baking powder
- 1/2 tsp. of sugar
- 1 egg
- 1/3 + 1 tbsp. of milk
- 2/3 tbsp. of butter, melted
- 1/2 tsp. of cayenne powder or Cajun seasoning
- 1/3 cup of Parmesan cheese
- 1/3 cup of diced crab meat

wwwwwwwwwwwwwwwwwwwwwwww

How to Cook:

i. In a bowl mix together flour and baking powder; in another bowl, mix together sugar, egg, milk, and butter.

ii. Fold the dry ingredients into the wet and stir, add cayenne powder or Cajun seasoning, cheese, and diced crab meat.

iii. Take 1/2 tbsp. worth of dough, form it into a ball, and fry until golden brown for a period of 1-3 minutes.

35. Happy as Clams Fritters

Serve: 12-15

Ingredient List:

- 1 1/2 cups of all-purpose flour
- 1/2 tsp. of baking powder
- 1/6 tsp. of salt and pepper
- 1 egg + 1 egg white
- 1/3 cup of minced clams
- 2 1/2 tbsp. of milk
- 1 tbsp. of minced shallot
- 1/2 tsp. of red pepper flakes

wwwwwwwwwwwwwwwwwwwwww

How to Cook:

i. In a bowl mix together flour, baking powder, salt, and pepper; in another bowl, mix together eggs, clams, milk, shallot, and pepper flakes.

ii. Fold the dry ingredients into the wet and stir; take 1/2 tbsp. worth of dough, form it into a ball, and fry until golden brown for a period of 1-3 minutes.

36. Appalachian Trail Fritters

Serve: 12

Ingredient List:

- 2/3 cup of all-purpose flour
- 2 tbsp. of cornmeal
- 2/3 tsp. of baking powder
- 1/4 tsp. of sugar
- 1 egg + 1 yolk
- 1/3 cup of buttermilk
- 1/2 tbsp. of butter, melted
- 1 tsp. of minced thyme
- 1 tsp. of minced oregano
- 1/2 tsp. of minced basil
- 1/3 cup of Parmesan cheese

wwwwwwwwwwwwwwwwwwwwwww

How to Cook:

i. In a bowl mix together flour and baking powder; in another bowl, mix together sugar, egg, milk, and butter.

ii. Fold the dry ingredients into the wet and stir, add herbs and cheese.

iii. Take 1/2 tbsp. worth of dough, form it into a ball, and fry until golden brown for a period of 1-3 minutes.

37. Florida Fritters

Serve: 12-15

Ingredient List:

- 1 1/2 cups of all-purpose flour
- 1/2 tsp. of baking powder
- 2 tbsp. of sugar
- 1 egg + 1 egg white
- 1/4 cup of orange juice
- 1/3 tbsp. of butter, melted
- 2 tsp. of orange peel

wwwwwwwwwwwwwwwwwwwwwww

How to Cook:

i. In a bowl mix together flour, baking powder, and sugar; in another bowl, mix together eggs, milk, orange juice, butter, and orange peel.

ii. Fold the dry ingredients into the wet and stir; take 1/2 tbsp worth of dough, form it into a ball, and fry until golden brown for a period of 1-3 minutes.

38. Gulf Coast Fritters

Serve: 12

Ingredient List:

- 3/4 cup of all-purpose flour
- 1 tbsp. of breadcrumbs or panko
- 1/3 tsp. of baking powder
- 1/4 tsp. of sugar
- 1 egg + 1 yolk
- 1/3 tbsp. of buttermilk
- 1/2 tsp. of lemon juice
- 1/4 tbsp. of butter, melted
- 1/2 cup of diced shrimp
- 1/2 cup of diced lobster meat
- 1 tbsp. of diced shallot
- 1 tbsp. of diced scallion

wwwwwwwwwwwwwwwwwwwwww

How to Cook:

i. In a bowl mix together flour, breadcrumbs/panko, and baking powder; in another bowl, mix together sugar, egg, buttermilk, butter, and lemon juice. Fold the dry ingredients into the wet and stir, add seafood and onions.

ii. Take 1/2 tbsp. worth of dough, form it into a ball, and fry until golden brown for a period of 1-3 minutes.

39. Autumns Apple Fritters

A classic comfort snack on fall days and cozy weekends at home!

Serve: 12

Ingredient List:

- 1 cup of all-purpose flour
- 1/3 tsp. of baking powder
- 1/4 tsp. of brown sugar
- 1 egg
- 2 tbsp. of milk
- 1 tsp. of butter, cut in
- 1/3 tsp. of cinnamon
- 1/2 tsp. of apple pie spice
- 1 1/2 cups of apple pie filling

wwwwwwwwwwwwwwwwwwwwww

How to Cook:

i. In a bowl mix together flour, baking powder, and brown sugar; in another bowl, mix together sugar, egg, milk, and butter.

ii. Fold the dry ingredients into the wet and stir, add seasonings and apple pie filling.

iii. Take 1/2 tbsp. worth of dough, form it into a ball, and fry until golden brown for a period of 1-3 minutes.

Dip Recipes

40. Herbed Blue Cheese Spread

Serve: 3-4 cups

Ingredient List:

- 2 8 oz. of blocks of cream cheese
- 1 cup of blue cheese
- 1 tbsp. of mayonnaise
- 1/3 tbsp. of each: thyme, basil, parsley, and mint
- 2 tsp. of white wine

wwwwwwwwwwwwwwwwwwwwwwww

How to Cook:

i. Stir together all the ingredients, transfer to an airtight container, and leave it to chill for at least a period of 20 minutes before serving.

41. Savory Onion Dip

Serve: 2-3 cups

Ingredient List:

- 1 tbsp. of butter
- 1/3 chopped sweet onion
- 1/3 cup of spinach
- 1 dash of black pepper
- 1 tub of sour cream
- 1 tbsp. of chives
- 1/2 tsp. of dill

wwwwwwwwwwwwwwwwwwwwwwww

How to Cook:

i. In a medium-sized pot over medium-high heat, sauté onions in melted butter then when about done add the spinach and sauté for a period of 1 more minute.

ii. Remove from the heat and add the remaining ingredients, mix well, transfer to a smaller air-tight bowl, and leave it to chill for a period of 1 hour.

42. South Florida Fish Dip

Serve: 3-4 cups

Ingredient List:

- 2 cups smoked fish
- 2 tbsp. of mayonnaise
- 3 tbsp. of sour cream
- 1/3 tbsp. of white wine
- 1/2 tbsp. of Cajun seasoning
- 1 - 2 tsp. of liquid smoke
- 1 tsp. of black pepper

How to Cook:

i. Stir together all the ingredients, transfer to an airtight container, and leave it to chill for at least a period of 20 minutes before serving.

43. Big Bend Shrimp Dip

Serve: approx. 3-4 cups

Ingredient List:

- 1/2 lbs. of diced medium-cooked shrimp: cleaned, detailed, and de-veined
- 1/2 diced shallot
- 1 tsp. of chives
- 2/3 cup of mayonnaise
- 1/2 cup of sour cream
- 1/2 tsp. of celery salt

wwwwwwwwwwwwwwwwwwwwwww

How to Cook:

i. In a bowl mix all the ingredients together and transfer to a serving bowl, let the bowl chill in the refrigerator for at least a period of 1 hour before serving.

44. Baked Spinach Dip

Serve: 3-4 cups

Ingredient List:

- 4 cups of spinach
- 1 cup of sour cream
- 1 tbsp. of minced garlic
- 1/4 cup of diced shallot
- 2 jars artichoke hearts
- 1/3 cup of pepper jack cheese
- 1/3 cup of cheddar cheese
- 1 jar red roasted peppers, drained
- 1/3 cup of heavy cream (for thinning, use only if needed)

wwwwwwwwwwwwwwwwwwwwwwww

How to Cook:

i. Preheat the oven to a temperature of 350°F and prepare a 9x11 casserole dish.

ii. Stir the ingredients together and bake for a period of 22-27 minutes.

45. Pimento Cheese Spread

Serve: 3-4 cups

Ingredient List:

- 1 cup of mayo
- 1 1/2 blocks (12 oz.) of cream cheese
- 1 package of shredded cheddar cheese
- 2/3 cup of pimento cheese
- 2 diced jalapenos (optional)
- 1/3 tbsp. of blue monde spice
- 1/4 tsp. of cayenne powder or turmeric

wwwwwwwwwwwwwwwwwwwwwwww

How to Cook:

i. Stir together all the ingredients, transfer the mixture to an airtight container and chill for at least a period of 20 minutes before serving.

46. Creamy Turnip Dip

Serve: approx. 3-4 cups

Ingredient List:

- 3 strips diced bacon
- 1 tsp. of butter
- 1/2 tsp. of onion powder
- 1/4 tsp. of garlic powder with parsley
- 1/3 cup of white cooking wine
- 2 cups of turnip greens
- 8 oz. of cream cheese
- 4 oz. of plain Greek yogurt
- 1 jar of roasted red peppers, drained
- 1 jar of sun-dried tomatoes, drained

wwwwwwwwwwwwwwwwwwwwwww

How to Cook:

i. Preheat the oven to a temperature of 300°F and prepare a 9x9 dish or another small dish.

ii. In a Dutch oven, cook the bacon pieces, remove, and let them drain; in the bacon grease add butter, onion powder, garlic, parsley powder, and wine (the wine will pick up the leftover bacon bits stuck to the pot).

iii. Let the mixture simmer for a few minutes then add turnip greens, cream cheese, yogurt, red peppers, sun-dried tomatoes, and bacon bits; stir well and bake at a temperature of 300°F for a period of 25-30 minutes.

47. Salsa Substitute

Serve: 3-4 cups

Ingredient List:

- 20 tomatillos
- 3 minced jalapenos
- 1 chopped onion
- 5 avocados
- 1 dash of salt
- 1/4 tsp. of lemon juice

wwwwwwwwwwwwwwwwwwwwww

How to Cook:

i. Boil the tomatillos for a period of 5-6 minutes, place all the ingredients in a food processor and blend till it is of a spread consistency.

48. Cauliflower Hummus

Serve: 3-4 cups

Ingredient List:

- 4 cups of chopped cauliflower
- 1 can of chickpeas, washed and drained
- 1 tbsp. of olive oil
- 1/2 tbsp. of lemon juice
- 1/4 tsp. of turmeric or smoked paprika
- 1/3 tbsp. of thyme

wwwwwwwwwwwwwwwwwwwwwww

How to Cook:

i. To roast the cauliflower: spread it out on a tray, drizzle it with olive oil, and bake it for a period of 20 minutes at a temperature of 425°F.

ii. Put all ingredients into a food processor and blend until a desired hummus consistency is reached.

49. Beer Dip

Serve: 3-4 cups

Ingredient List:

- 1 12 oz. of dark ale
- 1 cup of spicy mustard
- 3/4 tbsp. of mustard powder
- 1 tbsp. of brown sugar
- 2/3 tbsp. of apple cider vinegar
- 2/3 tbsp. of soy sauce or Worcester sauce

wwwwwwwwwwwwwwwwwwwwwww

How to Cook:

i. Let the ale simmer until it has been reduced by half, remove it from the heat and add the remaining ingredients, let the beer dip cool, and serve.

50. Lima Bean Guac

Serve: 3-4 cups

Ingredient List:

- 2 cups of lima beans
- 1 avocado
- 1 tsp. of onion powder
- 1/4 cup of lime juice
- 2 chopped and seeded jalapenos

wwwwwwwwwwwwwwwwwwwwwwww

How to Cook:

i. Boil the beans until they are tender, remove and rinse, stick them in the food processor along with the remaining ingredients, and pulse until a desired dip consistency is reached.

Author's Afterthoughts

thank you FOR YOUR ORDER

Practice makes perfect in the same way that expressing gratitude paves the way to success because it allows you to become surrounded by people who know how much you value them in your journey. I've been blessed to have a loving family, amazing friends, and beautiful readers like you who support me and push me to constantly improve by trying out my recipes!

I'm so grateful that I'd like to give back to you and all of my readers by asking what kind of content you'd like to see more of. Is it a book on a particular cuisine or cooking style? Would you like me to work on more weeknight recipes? I'm excited to know what your thoughts are so I can start brainstorming on my next cookbook! I read all of my replies, reviews, and suggestions, so don't hesitate to leave me a comment because I WILL get to it and put it to good use in my writing and cooking.

Thanks a bunch!

Rola Oliver

Printed in Great Britain
by Amazon